"God, Please Save Me "

Sr. Mary Rose McGeady

Covenant House

DEDICATED
to the 400,000 children
we have had the privilege of serving
these past 26 years — kids who were
scared, cold, hungry, alone and most of all,
desperate to find someone who cared.
We are honored to have helped.

Table of Contents

Introduction

If God didn't have such good ears, Covenant House might be empty tonight.

You see, all over the country tonight, there are kids who are alone and tired and scared. And in the dark, they whisper, "God, please save me. Please, God."

If they stood on a street corner and screamed this plea ... if they made signs ... if they took out ads in newspapers with this message, people like you and I would respond.

How could we not respond?

But they don't. They don't trust the world enough to do that. They don't trust adults enough to do that.

So they whisper it ... "God, please save me" ... and God alone hears. And when He hears, He sends them to me.

I am Sister Mary Rose McGeady. For eight years, I have been President of Covenant House, the largest system of emergency shelters — and the most important source of second chances — for homeless kids in America. We serve 1,400 children a night — kids from all walks of life and from every part of the country.

It is my belief that the overwhelming majority of

those kids are here because at some point their lives became so horrible that they begged God to save them ... and He heard them.

It's a good thing He has such good ears.

Even after they get here, it takes a while before they will say anything loud enough for us to hear. When they finally do begin to talk, they tell stories of sexual abuse, physical assault and emotional violation by parents, stepparents or other adults in their lives.

They also tell us about what happened to them when they escaped from home and ended up on the streets. These stories are frightening enough to make me wonder how the kids survive even a few weeks in the land of pimps, pushers and pornographers.

Some of the kids simply don't survive.

This book is my attempt to tell the stories of some of our kids. I hope you will read it.

I have to warn you ahead of time, though, that these are not necessarily pretty stories. I have talked to so many kids, and heard so many stories, that I keep thinking I've heard the worst one and it will be easier from now on.

I'm always wrong.

After eight years, I'm still shocked by some of the things that happen to kids at the hands of their parents — the people to whom God entrusts His children. And the stories of what happens to kids on the streets are enough to make me wonder if the world doesn't hate kids.

But although these stories may not be pretty, they

are inspiring. If you read them, you will meet some of the most innocent, beautiful and hopeful kids. You will meet kids with courage and endurance and strength that boggles the mind.

You will meet kids who have lived through a hell that you and I can barely imagine ... and yet they still believe in heaven.

You will meet some of my most favorite people in all the world.

This year, Covenant House will serve 48,000 abused or neglected kids in cities all across America — in New York, Los Angeles, Ft. Lauderdale, New Orleans, Anchorage, Newark, Washington, D.C., Orlando, Atlantic City, Houston and our newest Covenant House in Detroit. And as you read this, we are also saving kids in shelters throughout Central America, as well as in Toronto, Vancouver and Mexico City (and soon, St. Louis and Oakland).

The fact is that Covenant House spends more to help homeless kids than the federal government. We give the kids a place to stay and warm food and clothes. We make sure they get medical care if they need it. We help them heal from the incredible pain they've suffered. We help them start over with school or a job or a permanent place to live.

I hope that after you've read these stories about some of my favorite people, you'll want to help us. Quite frankly, a large part of my job is to raise the money to keep all our Covenant House shelters open. On behalf of the kids, I have to ask, and ask, and ask again for people to support this refuge for street children.

I have to keep asking because I know that somewhere out there tonight, God is hearing an anguished voice. He's trying hard to understand the words through the sobs.

And when He hears, "God, please save me," He's going to send that child to me.

Sister Mary Rose McGeady
June 9, 1998

No stranger I, to death.
He lives with me each day.
He tempts me with my grave,
and hides the price I'll pay.

A poem from
a street kid

*"The love of God
is creative to infinity."*

St. Vincent de Paul

Chapter 1

"I just want another chance," he said.

The ghost arrived on our doorstep around eight o'clock that first night, skin and bones and pasty white skin swimming inside a bunch of old rags.

It was hard to tell his age in the twilight. I searched for his eyes to get an idea, but they showed nothing and said nothing. They just lurked inside, sunk deep in their sockets, hiding from the light.

From the way his tired body slumped forward, I could tell his spirit was already dead, and he was marking time until his body caught up. He didn't have long to wait. If ever I saw a kid who was "too late to help," this kid was it.

We wrapped him into our arms, and rushed him inside our crisis shelter, praying very hard.

For three days, he was in agony. He threw up, he couldn't sleep. He had convulsions. And tears. So many tears.

And finally, in a brief lull between spasms, The Ghost (as I came to think of him) spoke. His voice was a hoarse whisper. It was frightening.

"My mother got cancer when I was 10," he said.

"I'd never been close to my father. I don't think he ever really wanted me — but he loved Mom.

"After she died, he went over the edge. Knocked me around, told me I was a worthless piece of junk, that I should have died instead of her." He paused, closing his eyes.

"Anyway, that's when I began hangin' out on corners, just to be away from him. I got into shooting dope in sixth grade.

"Then he kicked me out. That was five years ago. I've been on the street ever since.

"Now I just want the world to leave me alone. I want to die."

Turning in his bed, The Ghost faced the wall. I reached out to touch his back gently, afraid that the weight of my hand would hurt his tortured body.

Somehow, we got him through the rest of withdrawal, coaxed him to eat, hand-led him to counseling. He went along like a zombie: passive, mute, expressionless.

"We're doing everything we can," I remember thinking. "But nothing's working. This kid may be too far gone...."

Then, one Tuesday evening, something happened I will never, ever forget.

"I've decided something," The Ghost said, looking into my eyes for the first time.

"I've decided I want to live," he said.

"I really do," he said.

It wasn't an easy road. For days and weeks and months, Michael fought the drug addiction rattling inside him. Where once heroin had been his answer, his fastest and surest escape from a life in which no one cared about him or wanted him, it now was his curse. Many nights we held his hand as he rocked and cried in his bed, fighting to hold onto his body and his new dream to stay alive.

"Please, God, help me," he began to cry as the time wore on. "I'm sorry about what I did ... I just want another chance."

Finally, one day, the breakthrough came and the curse of his addiction lifted. It was like the sun suddenly decided to come out in his life — 18 years too late, but finally there. Michael was so overwhelmed with joy, he just sat outside on our steps and cried very quiet and private tears of relief.

After that, Michael's recovery moved quickly. He was a very bright kid. We helped him get his high school diploma and apply for scholarships to college.

That was last year. Today, he dropped in to say hello. And my memory of The Ghost came flashing back.

Michael told me that he's working as a veterinary assistant, going to college full time — and earning straight As!

"Thank you," he kept saying to everyone he bumped into. "I really want to thank you," he kept repeating over and over again.

"Thank you," I kept saying back to him. I don't know which one of us was happier.

I wish you could have been there. That first night, and today, too. I mean, I know that it's not always easy to read these letters. It's tough to hear about kids who are lost and hurting and desperate, and may never ever know anything else but abandonment and hurt and desperation.

And God knows you have your own concerns and troubles and worries. But, I met someone today who was given a new life by you. Nothing less. He owes his rebirth, and his life, to wonderful people like you.

I don't know how else to say it, other than to say it like that. In our too-fast, too-complicated, too-material-istic, too-self-absorbed world — you again reached out and made the biggest and perhaps ultimately, only, dif-ference that really matters. You gave someone his life back.

I can't thank you enough for what you have given to Michael and the hundreds and hundreds of other kids standing at our doors tonight. Perhaps it might be enough, I hope, for you to know that we are all eternally grateful and thankful for you, and that we never stop thanking God you found us.

Never.

Thank you again, so much. And please remember, you are always in my prayers....

If

If all lips spoke the truth,
All pride was cast aside,
Greed was packed and stored away,
And jealousy subside.
If love could rule the universe,
Kindness was sown to every race,
Then one could glance into a mirror
And view God in his face....

> *Written by a 16-year-old*
> *girl on the street*

Chapter 2

*"I'm not even sure
where I was born," she said.*

"Where are you from?"

"I don't know," she said.

"Where's your mother?"

"She's dead," she said.

"How did she die?"

"I don't know," she said.

"Do you have a father?"

She opened her mouth to answer me again, in the same beaten voice that dripped from her, but this time the words just wouldn't come out. She just kept standing there, a small and tormented and very lonely figure, swallowing hard, staring at her shoes, brushing tears away from her eyes.

She was very special. I could tell that right away. In our world of lost and lonely and hurting kids, she stood out right away as the most lost and hurting of all — a kid who is utterly and totally disconnected from anyone or anyplace. An innocent completely lacking in identity. A kid who has been forced to go through life not really knowing who she is, where she came from and how she ever got there.

I took a deep breath, laid my hand on her and tried

not to show how much I was hurting and worrying inside.

"Here, let's go sit over here," I said pointing to a table in our shelter. I thought I'd just spend a moment talking to her, telling her how glad we were she found us and how much we wanted to help her, but she surprised me. As hard as it was for her to tell me her story, she wanted to. I think she had to....

"I ... I actually do have a father," she said.

"He's right here in New York. That's why I'm here," she said.

"Where were you before?" I asked.

"In Chicago. I ... like I said, I don't really have a home. I'm not even sure where I was born. I've lived in foster homes my whole life since I was four. But they were really bad, Sister. I couldn't take it anymore. So I left. During the last couple of years I've been living in an abandoned building in Chicago with a bunch of other kids my age." (She looked about 17 to me.)

"That must be really hard," I said, thinking of how cold and lonely and terrifying that kind of life is for a kid.

"It's OK," she said. "I mean, at least I felt safe there. At least I had some people that were like my family."

I winced inside again.

"A couple of weeks ago, I was able to find out where my father is living. I didn't know before. I hadn't seen him since I was four. So I wrote him a letter, and asked him if I could visit him. He said I could.

That's why I came to New York. I hitchhiked all the **way. It took me** a week."

Jenny reached down and grabbed the backpack she had been carrying, and then softly tapped it a few times. The tears began flowing a little faster.

"What happened next?" I asked.

"It was awful," she said. "He didn't want to see me, Sister. He just wanted my money. He's a crack addict.

"I ... I can't believe this happened." And then Jenny broke down and cried. I felt my heart breaking too.

I really don't know what's going to happen to Jenny. Jenny is poised at that edge between childhood and adulthood and she has no base from which to make that leap.

She has no fond memories. No photos of her family. No birth certificate. No hometown.

Her father is a crack addict. Her mother is dead.

Everything she has is in one overnight bag. And it is the most neatly packed bag I have ever seen. (It was amazing, really, when we took her to her room to get a good night's sleep and we saw her unpack. Even though she was homeless, everything in her pack was clean and neatly folded. She even had four or five packages of chewing gum in each compartment. "I have to," she explained when I asked her why. "I never know when I'll get a chance to brush my teeth, so I like to be prepared." She really is a remarkable kid....)

I don't know whether to think that she is quite

remarkable in her ability to cope. Or whether to wonder what kind of heartbreak is concealed behind that neat, organized exterior.

I do know that we will be here for her now, to be the family she has never had, to provide the anchor she has never known.

It's going to take a while. But some day soon, I hope, after we have given her the love and counseling and support she desperately needs (in essence, after we've helped Jenny "reclaim" her life), we will then help Jenny rebuild it in our Rights of Passage program. In "Rights" we'll help get Jenny everything she needs to pass from childhood to adulthood, the things she so richly deserves but was robbed of — an education, job training, independent living skills — complete with a caring mentor who will guide her and encourage her every step of the way.

It's a long, long journey ahead for Jenny. But I already know she's one of those kids who's going to make it. I just know it.

Thank you, as always, for being there for Jenny, and the 1,399 other kids we'll see tonight. I know you have concerns of your own and bills to pay and family to worry about. I know it's not always easy being a loving and guiding parent to the 1,400 kids we see every night.

But please know, every second, how much it means to me and to these kids. In a world where beautiful and innocent kids like Jenny are all too often simply discarded and forgotten, it's your hands and heart that give them hope. It's your love that makes the difference. I can't say it often enough or loudly enough. Your prayers and support mean everything to them. And to me.

Thank you, thank you, thank you for caring about them as much as you do. I never stop thanking God you found us.

Dear Heavenly Father,
Please give me the strength to go on through my
stay at Covenant House. Give me the wisdom and
the knowledge to do what is right and not wrong.
And please give me the strength to make the right
decisions about the things that occur. I know I
haven't been making the right decisions, but I'd
like to better that. Life has not been easy for me
through these times, but I know that you will give
me the strength to go on for I do believe in you and
all you say and do. Amen.

A prayer written
by a kid in our
Covenant House Chapel

Chapter 3

"I've been on the street since I was 13."

"I had to run away from Satan, so I ran away from home."

A cold, freezing rain washed over my eyes as I stood on the steps of our newest Covenant House shelter in Vancouver.

I couldn't tell if the girl sitting on the steps beneath me was kidding or serious, although I guess I really knew the answer. My head knew she was telling me the truth, but my heart just didn't want to accept it yet.

"What do you mean?" I asked her.

Julie looked at me with sad and weary eyes, as if she couldn't believe what she was about to tell me.

"Oh, you know," she said. "Uhmmm ... my parents were devil worshippers," she said. "They were Satan lovers," she said, her voice trailing off. I could almost feel the disgust and grief in her voice....

"I almost can't believe what they did," she said. "I mean, when I was eight, they decided to join this Satanic Cult. There were scary people everywhere," she said, her eyes filling with disgust.

"I kept hoping one day they'd snap out of it. I kept thinking this was just a big nightmare, and it would end some day," she said. "But my parents started doing the same horrible stuff the cult leaders were doing.

"I ... I don't even want to tell you about it," she said, her eyes beginning to fill with tears. "I woke up every morning scared, I went through every day scared, I went to bed every night scared.

"When I got older I tried to tell my parents I hated this. I told them I was scared. I told them I couldn't take it anymore," she said. "They just told me to shut up ... do what the leaders told me ... to accept Satan."

She stopped for a moment to look up at me. I think she just wanted to make sure I was hearing what she was saying, and believing what she was saying and that I really and truly cared about what she was saying.

"Please don't think I'm crazy too," her eyes were screaming out to me. "Please, Sister, I know this sounds awful, but don't think I'm awful too," her eyes were saying. "I need someone to believe me," her eyes said.

It wasn't a look of anger anymore, but of profound sadness and grief. I could tell she could barely believe the words coming out of her mouth.

She cleared her throat for a second, then began to speak again. Deliberately. So I didn't miss a word.

"I tried staying with them, but I couldn't take it anymore. I mean, I was scared to death. I didn't know what to do. I thought I was going to die there.

"So I did the only thing I could. I ran away."

Her eyes looked up at me again. This time, I could see the beginnings of a flood of tears forming on her already-wet face. I wanted to reach out and hug her right there, but I knew it wasn't the time.

"That must have been awful," I said. Her eyes gave me a nod, and then asked me to go on.

"It must have been tough out on the street," I said. "Were you all alone?" I asked, as her eyes nodded yes. "How old are you, about 16 or 17?" I asked.

"Seventeen," she mumbled softly into the steps.

"I've been on the streets since I was 13," she mumbled.

"And it's been really bad," she said.

"I mean, you don't have any idea how scary it was," she said. "I didn't know where to go, I didn't have anything to eat. I used to just walk the streets at night, trying to keep warm, hoping I wouldn't die."

I opened my mouth again to tell her how sorry I was that she had suffered so much, but she stopped me before I could get the words out. She had something she wanted me to understand.

If I live to be one hundred, I'll never forget it.

"But you know what," she said. "As bad as it was, running away was the best thing I ever did," she said.

"It ... was ... the ... best ... thing ... I ... ever ... did," she repeated, slowly and solemnly before breaking down in tears.

I put my hand on her heaving shoulder, and patted her as gently as I could. "I understand," I said. "I'm so glad you came to us," I said. "We're going to take care of you," I said.

"I think it was the best thing she ever did," I said quietly to God. "I promise you I'll make sure she's OK for now," I said.

I'm still having a little trouble believing this whole story. I know I spend so many letters telling you about how awful the street is for kids ... and it is. How so many of them are dying out there ... and they are. How thousands and thousands of children desperately need someone to save them this minute ... and they do.

But as hard as this might be to believe, sometimes it actually is better for a kid to run away. As hard as it is to comprehend, right now there are thousands of kids like Julie who are so desperate, and live in such awful situations, that the only way they will ever find help and hope is to leave home.

Can you imagine what that must be like? To live in a world that is so awful, that the streets (streets that are dark and foreboding and lonely and scary) become a better choice. My heart aches for these kids. I know God has a special place in His infinite heart for them. Their pain — their torture — their misery — is almost beyond comprehension.

And as I stood there on a rainy, cold morning in Vancouver, I couldn't help but think that we were just in time for Julie. Thanks to friends like you, we just opened the new shelter in Vancouver. But even before we officially opened, kids like Julie began sleeping on the steps, waiting to get in.

"Since I left, I've been living on the streets," Julie told me. "It's hard, but still better than home.

"I make some money by reciting my poetry. I stop people on the sidewalk and tell them a poem for a dollar. It works out OK. But sometimes I don't make any money, and I don't have any place to sleep."

Thank you for being here. We're going to help Julie find a real home. And in the meantime, she has food, clothes and a safe, warm place to sleep. It's hard to explain how much those things mean to a kid who has been surviving on the streets.

*"Covenant House is like a family, with
all a family's ups and downs. But the
really great thing about being here is
that I'm never lonely anymore. There's
always someone here, no matter what
time, to talk to. And that makes a big
difference when you're trying to build a
life for yourself."*

> *James, 18,*
> *a Covenant House*
> *resident*

Chapter 4

"I live below the city," he said.
"In the tunnels."

The boy sat beside me, hunched over his chair, cradling a pencil in one hand and a beaten up sketch pad in the other.

He was one of those enigma kids, the type who comes to us carrying sad and desperate eyes and a secret hurt that is hidden deep inside, but is so searing and overwhelming that you can literally see it piercing through their body.

"Hi" was all he could quietly mumble when we opened our shelter door to him this morning.

"Can I stay here for a while?" he asked.

After we had welcomed him at our New York shelter and told him how much we cared, and let him know we were here to help him, we led his tired body and heart over to a sofa, where he could find a moment's rest.

For the next couple of hours he sat there, eyes closed, a tattered old backpack near his feet, his pencil and sketch pad on his lap.

I had a million other things I needed to do, and a thousand other things on my mind and a hundred other kids I needed to talk to, but I decided to park myself on the sofa beside him and wait for the right time. I couldn't risk the chance we might lose him.

Finally, after what seemed like an eternity, he opened his eyes. They were two of the emptiest, lost eyes I have ever seen.

"You seem very tired," I said trying to make a connection. His eyes blinked slowly in agreement.

"I'm really glad you found us," I said. "What is your name?"

The question seemed to surprise him, as if no one had cared enough about who he was to ask him his name before.

"My name is Michael," he said in words barely above a whisper. "Mike."

"Where are you from?" I asked.

He closed his eyes again for a moment, wondering if he should even answer. "You probably won't believe me," he said, a little embarrassed.

"Try me," I said. "I'd like to help you. We all would."

He stared straight at me, with that unmistakable "should-I-or-shouldn't-I" look kids get sometimes, like when they're perched on the edge of a diving board contemplating if now is the time to jump off for that first time. I was smiling back as hard as I could, trying to urge him to jump off. After what seemed like an eternity, he did.

"I live below the city," he said. "In the tunnels."

"Right here," he said, handing me his sketch pad.

There, in elaborately drawn page after page, were

dark and vivid scenes from his world, a place I had never seen before.

"Is this where you live?" I asked, pointing to a drawing of a dark room littered with boxes and what looked like an old chair. "Yes," his head nodded.

"Is this your mother?" I asked, pointing to a drawing of a woman, face smeared with dirt, her arms around a boy who was clearly meant to be him. "Yes," he nodded.

"Is your father there, too?"

For the first time he pulled back and cringed a little, and his eyes shut tight.

"Do you want to talk about it?" I asked. He shook his head no. "I don't have a father," was all he would say.

I placed my hand on his shoulder, and comforted him for a moment. I could tell he'd told me as much as he could right now. The talking and remembering were getting to be too much for him.

"We really hope you stay," I said. "I want you to stay," I said for extra emphasis. "Do you want something to eat, and then maybe a chance to sleep?"

His lips broke out into a half smile, and his eyes clenched. "Yeah," he whispered. "Thanks."

I waved over to Jim, one of our super-great counselors (all our Covenant House staff is great, I must say in my own unbiased opinion!) and asked him to help Mike. "Take extra care of Mike," I said loud enough so he could hear me. "He's a great kid."

Mike smiled a little smile, and nodded thanks as he

walked off down the hallway. Even now, 10 hours later, I can't stop thinking about him.

I mean, I think Mike is my official-unofficial "Lent kid" for this year (I'm convinced every year God sends me one extra special kid to remind me what Lent is all about).

I think Lent is all about self-examination, and things we must ask ourselves, and reckoning, and looking in the mirror to see if we like what's staring back at us.

(I'm not the world's biggest fan of Lent. In fact, I really don't like it ... it's not something we're supposed to like, I guess.)

It's a time to reflect on how we use the goods of the world, and how we deal with our relationships. It's a time to think about whether we're really trying to live a life of love, a time to look under the hood of our souls to make sure everything's running all right and see where the defects are.

Lent is also about resolutions to turn our lives around, and then beginning the process of dealing with those resolutions....

Easy? It's not, and it's not supposed to be. It's not easy spending 40 days staring into the mirrors of our souls, scrutinizing, writing checklists, grading performance. It's never easy asking ourselves if we're really being as good as we want to be, as virtuous, as steadfast, as understanding. But it's a good time for us, I think. Lent is a time when we are asked to draw ourselves closer to God.

Mike? And other kids like Mike? I think they know all about Lent, and what God intended for Lent, better than most of us ever will. Our kids live in a perpetual Lent ... a nonstop life of painful reckoning, questioning, excruciating self-examination, of losses.

"What is wrong with me?" our kids find themselves asking, and asking and asking. "Why am I living like this ... why doesn't anyone love me ... am I suffering because I don't deserve anything better?"

Sometimes, as in Mike's case, the reckoning and self-examination is so powerful and painful, they can only share it by drawing it out on a sketch pad. Saying the words, and hearing the words, hurts too much.

Lent is truly in their hearts every minute of their lives.

Of course, it's not hard to see God in their sad eyes and tired faces. I know, I just know, you'd see Him there, too.

Could I ask you two special favors for our kids this Lent? First, maybe you could make a point to say a prayer for our kids every day. Please pray for the 1,400 kids who thankfully have found help in one of our shelters, and for the kids who are still searching, still living in subways, still immersed in an excruciating, non-stop Lent that seems without end. Your prayers would mean a lot to these kids, and to me. Thank you for that.

And maybe you could also help our kids with a special Lenten gift today? Our needs are really great right now. Thanks to your incredible kindness and prayers and support, we'll help more than 48,000 kids

this year. All of them searching. All of them hoping.
All of them wondering if there might finally be a better
world for them.

Your love makes all the difference for all of them.
You really do. We couldn't be here for these kids without you. Maybe you could help again now?

Thank you so much for reading this letter and praying for our kids. We never, ever stop thanking God you
found us. Never! Especially during Lent....

"On the street I saw a girl cold and shivering in a thin dress, with little hope of a decent meal. I became angry and said to God: 'Why did You permit this? Why don't You do something about it?' For a while God said nothing. That night He replied quite suddenly: 'I certainly did something about it. I made you.'"

Chapter 5

"They're cigarette burns,"
she said softly.
"I got them from my mother."

"My arms never forget, Sister. Never."

She rubbed her arms self-consciously from her elbows to her wrists, letting her words and her anger sink in, and then thrust them before me.

Her thin, tiny arms were covered with small, round scars. Some were old and faint. Others were new and raw.

"This one hurt the most," she said, gently rubbing an area on her left forearm that was covered with a group of sores. "I can still feel it," she said.

"What happened?" I asked. "Do you want to tell me about it?" I asked. I already knew how the scars got there. I knew what they were. I've seen them too many times in my life. But I wanted to give Linda the chance to tell me.

I could tell from the tears forming in her eyes that she really wanted to tell me.

"They're cigarette burns," she said softly to the floor. "I got them from my mother," she said. Her voice was barely a whisper now, dripping with sadness and more than a little embarrassment. (It's a common and heartbreaking reaction among kids who've been severely abused. They're so racked with self-doubt and self-loathing, that they're ashamed to share too much of their pain. As if their scars are their fault, as if the abuse was their doing.)

"I used to get them all the time," she said, whispering. "Whenever my mom got real mad, she would burn me on the arm.

"I finally got tired of it," she said. "And I ran away and told people I was homeless. I wanted to get away from my mother, but I didn't want to get her in trouble.

"So I got put into a home," she said. "That was five years ago," she said. "I was 11 back then," she said.

"What happened next?" I asked.

"I ran into my mother on the street a few months ago," she said, tears beginning to flow down her face. "She seemed real happy to see me. She hugged me and told me she loved me. She said she was so worried about me, and asked me to come home. So I ran away back to her," she said.

Linda paused for a long time and swallowed hard. I could see a million memories and thoughts and regrets and dreams all racing behind her wet eyes at once. It was pretty obvious from the anguish written on her face what was coming next....

"It was really great for a couple of weeks," she said. "But then my mom started going crazy again when she got mad at me," she said. "She started doing this to me again," she said, pointing to two of the fresher marks on her arm.

"I will never forget what she's done to me," she said, her anger returning in her voice for a second before it gave way to silence again. Slowly her body began to shake, and then she began to cry.

It was not a soft cry, but a long, mournful, angry burst of agony and emotion. I reached out and hugged her for a moment, her tears growing longer and louder, shaking me and the scores of kids and staff who were assembled on our Intake floor. (Our shelter is busy, fast-paced, frenetic and noisy. It takes a lot to stop everyone in their tracks, if only for a second. This morning, Linda's crying did.)

It took me 10 minutes to calm Linda down. During that time, a million questions were racing through my head. I wanted to ask her what had happened to her father, suspecting that he and Linda's mother had gone separate ways a long time ago (I found out later he had). I wanted to ask if there was anyone else — an aunt, a relative, a grandparent — who might take Linda into their home (I found out later there wasn't). And I wanted to know if Linda had called and reported her mother (I found out later she had).

But at that moment, I just let her tears do enough talking for both of us. I think it was the first time in years — maybe the first time ever — that Linda had actually felt that someone cared.

I don't know how this is all going to turn out. I wish I could tell you something different, but I can't.

The wounds on Linda's arms are awful. They will take a long time to heal. Maybe they'll never go away.

I don't know.

But the real scars, the ones that can never be forgotten, are the ones inside. In her heart.

Linda's heart is worn out from being hurt and abandoned, and then trusting again and then being hurt again. It has big scars. Really big scars.

And I remember a parable I once heard about a wise man who was asked how to fix a gap in a ring. He said the gap could never be repaired. But he could put a jewel across the gap and make it something beautiful again.

That's the way I feel about Linda. You and I can't ever fix that gap in Linda's heart. But we can put a jewel of love there to make it beautiful again. With God's help, we can convince Linda that there are people who will love her. People whom she can trust.

Thank you for being here for Linda. I thank God every single day that you found us.

Dear God,
I just want someone to love me, someone to talk
to when I need to talk. Someone to cry on when I
need to cry. Most of all someone to love me and
walk as far as they wish through my life. Amen.

A prayer written
by a kid in our
Covenant House chapel

Chapter 6

"It was do that or die," he told me.

"He kept trying to stuff the $500 into my shirt pocket," the scrawny kid said to me this morning.

"That was the toughest part, Sister. I wanted to grab the money, but I couldn't. I knew I couldn't.

"I really could have used that money, though," he said shaking his head slowly. "I really, really needed it."

Paul looked at me, and peered into my eyes, wondering and fearing and worrying what I'd do next.

He had come to us one month ago, a boy at the end of his rope looking for one last chance to live.

From the second he fell inside, it was painfully clear that he was in a little more pain, a little more trouble, a little more agony than most of the kids we see here every day.

From the way he walked, we knew right away that he was a child of war; a beaten, tired, road-weary fighter from the battlefields of America's dead-end streets. From the way he looked at us, we knew that the fight to live had been long and hard and all-consuming.

He was one of those kids who comes to us still alive, but just barely. Whatever material possessions he owned, he wore on his back. Whatever spirit and heart he had left, he wore on his sleeve.

Fortunately for us and Paul, there was an unmistakable pride and courage on that sleeve. I'm sure it's what had kept him alive.

"That must have been really hard to turn that money down," I said to Paul this morning.

"I'm sure the temptation must have been incredible.

"What were you thinking about when that happened?" I asked.

Paul looked up at me, and tried to stop the tears forming in his eyes. He kept blinking, but he couldn't hold them back. They started coming.

"I was thinking that for the first time in my life, I think I have a chance to actually have a life," he said.

"And if I took that money, and did what the man wanted me to do, I was going to be throwing my last chance away," he said.

"I understand," I said.

"I'm so very proud of you, Paul," I said.

"I know how hard that must have been."

As I stood there, I thought back again to that first moment I had seen Paul, one month ago. The journey to this moment had been longer and harder than for most kids. It's a miracle really that Paul had finished the journey at all....

"I've been on the streets forever," he had told me that first day in our shelter.

"My stepfather started sexually abusing me when I was a kid," he said. "I couldn't take it another day ... I had to get out," he said. "I didn't want to run, but I didn't have a choice," he said.

"How old were you, Paul?" I had asked him that first day last month. "Sixteen? Fifteen?"

"Eleven," he had said.

"Eleven?" I repeated.

"Yeah, eleven."

No matter how many times I tell people that there are kids this young on the streets, many don't believe me. But Paul was just the latest proof.

Eleven years old! On the streets of a major city by himself. Can you imagine? It makes me want to cry.

Paul survived ... but it was the most awful kind of survival. Scared, alone, without money and friends, Paul began to sell himself to stay alive.

"It was do that or die," he told me. "I wanted to live. So I did it ... for five years," he said.

"I hated myself doing it ... it was awful," he said.

"But I wanted to live," he said, pleading with me to understand. "I didn't have a choice.

"I thought about killing myself. I couldn't take it anymore," he said.

"But then someone told me about Covenant House."

Since Paul found Covenant House a month ago, his life has literally been reborn. Despite all the pain in his past, despite the enormous hurdles he faces to build a future, Paul has slowly begun to build a life for himself.

And today, this morning, he overcame his biggest hurdle yet.

"So, what did you say to that man when he handed you the money?" I asked Paul this morning.

"I told him to keep it," he said.

"I told him I was too good for that stuff," he said.

"I told him that I was trying to get a regular job. And that he should take a hike," he said, a little smile breaking onto his face.

He is just 17, a beautiful kid who has been through a war that none of us can ever really comprehend.

And today, finally, he turned his back on his old life, and in the process turned his life around.

"I told him I was too good for that stuff," he said.

Thank you for being there for Paul. Thank you for being there for him last month when he walked through our doors needing someone to care. And thank you for being there in his heart this morning on that street-corner, when he looked his past squarely in the eye and said, "No ... enough ... I'm too good for that stuff ... I'm going to build a better life."

You helped save a kid this past month. Indeed, you've helped save a bunch of them. Thank you so much for all you do and all you've done.

I truly do thank God every minute that you found us!

Help Me

Help me, Dear Lord,
    as I travel towards You.
There are many detours
    which will try to distract
    me away from You.
Help me as I travel my path
    to cherish the parents You gave me.
Help me to do my best in all my endeavors
    whether I may win or lose.
Help me never to lose hope
    though there may be difficult times.
Help me to choose good friends.
Help me to choose the right mate,
    so that I may have a happy family someday.
Help me, though I may fall,
    to continue on my journey towards You.
Help me, Dear Lord.
I want so much to be with You. Amen.

                            Written by a
                            Covenant House kid

Chapter 7

"I used to be from somewhere, but I'm not from anywhere anymore," she said.

"I heard that you could help me," she said.

"Maybe you could just let me have a sandwich, and I'll get out of your hair," she said.

"I really don't want to get in your way."

I looked into her sad, no-one-loves-me eyes, and felt a stake piercing through my heart. She was a little kid, maybe 14 or 15 or 16 dressed in blue jeans and a sweatshirt that should have been thrown into a trash heap months ago. She was one of those street urchins we see so often, the kind of vagabond/bump-around/hard-knocks kid who mysteriously appears at our doorstep all of a sudden, covered with filth and oozing neglect.

I actually had a hard time guessing her age, there was so much dirt and pain smeared across her face.

But there was no mistaking her sweetness and her goodness. Even in the twilight of an early spring evening, we could see those qualities from a mile away. You would have loved her the second you laid eyes on her....

"Maybe I could even get a little something to drink too," she said. "If it wouldn't be a problem?"

"Please, come in," I said. "We've got plenty of food. Please, we're glad you are here," I said.

She tried to smile back, but I could tell she wasn't too used to smiling. She nodded a small nod, and quickly walked in.

"There's a cafeteria down the hall," I said. "Why don't we just take a minute to wash our hands and get cleaned up, and I'll take you there myself," I said. "My name is Sister Mary Rose — what's yours?" I said.

"Dana," she said.

"Where are you from?" I said.

"Nowhere," she said.

"What do you mean?" I said.

"Well ... I mean I used to be from somewhere, but I'm not from anywhere anymore," she said. "Is this the way to the cafeteria?" she said.

I took her by the hand, and led her to a sink and a bar of soap, where she could clean off the layers of dirt camped out on her hands and arms. It wasn't a simple cleaning — it was a good forty-five seconds before I could see her red, chafed skin underneath. Once her hands were dried, I hurried her to the cafeteria, where hot soup and sandwiches were lined neatly on the countertops.

Dana grabbed three of each, rushed politely over to the first empty table, and dove in. It took her all of five minutes to clean off the entire tray.

"Thanks a lot," she said. "That was really good," she said. "Maybe I can come back again," she said, half-asking, half-telling, totally hoping I'd say yes.

"You're welcome to stay now," I said. "We've got plenty of clean beds (plenty was a tiny exaggeration, because we're crammed with kids right now, but I was **trying** to convince her **to stay as hard as** I could), and you're welcome."

She fidgeted with the napkin, not quite knowing what to say. I could tell she was beginning to get interested....

"Tell me a little about yourself," I said. "How old are you?"

"Sixteen," she said.

"Is there someone we can call to let them know you're here," I said.

"There used to be," she said. "But not anymore."

"What do you mean," I said. "I'd like to help you," I said.

For the longest time, Dana looked at me, twisting her napkin, trying to decide a hundred things all at once. Should I talk? Or should I go? Can I trust this lady? What is this place? Why am I here? How did this happen? Is this someone I can believe in? Where am I going to sleep tonight if I don't sleep here? What should I do? A hundred questions ... all of them way too serious and heartbreaking and urgent for a 16-year-old kid to have to worry about.

Finally, the tears began to form in her eyes, and she decided to take a chance. Dana decided to trust in us.

"I used to live in a real house," she said. "I had a mother and a father and five brothers," she said. "That was a long time ago," she said.

"Then, last year, my dad decided to leave. He just walked out one day ... he didn't even tell me he was going anywhere ... he just left.

"My mother ... my mother couldn't take it anymore. She tried to get a job ... but it all got to be too much.

"About two months ago, she sat me down and told me I had to leave. 'You're 16, Dana,' she said. 'You're the oldest ... I can't afford all of you ... you're going to have to leave.'

"I looked at her like she was kidding. I mean, leave for what, Sister? Go where? I'm 16 ... it's not like I know a million places to go.

"But my mother kept telling me I had to get out," Dana said. " 'You can make it, Dana,' my mother said. 'You're strong like me. Pack up your things. I'm sorry, you have to go.' "

As she poured out her story, the tears began rolling down Dana's cheeks in streams. They were the angry, pained, disbelieving tears of a 16-year-old girl who suddenly found herself all alone, on the street, by herself. I grabbed her hand and told her again how glad I was she had found us. She cried some more, and tried to keep on talking....

"At first ... at first I thought I could make it. I met a boy on the street the first day. I thought maybe I could live with him.

"But ... but that didn't work out ... it ... it didn't work out."

"Where have you been living?" I asked.

"Around," she said. "You know, places," she said, street kid shorthand for alleys, subways, park benches and any other place where a kid can find a spot to sleep.

"We'd love to have you stay with us," I said. "We've got plenty of room," I said.

"I think I'd like that," she said. And then she began to sob uncontrollably. It was a long time before she could stop.

I made sure our staff took extra special care of Dana tonight. We got her some brand-new pajamas, and I made sure she got a room right near one of her counselors, so she could see someone by her all night.

I'm not sure how, or if, she'll be able to sleep tonight.

I mean, I know she's exhausted. She probably hasn't had a restful moment since she was kicked out of her home. But the questions pouring through her head, bouncing back and forth ... I'm sure they're keeping her up tonight.

"How did I ever end up here?" her mind must be asking her. "What did I do wrong? Am I going to always be alone? Am I ever going to be OK? Can I trust these people here? Can I ever trust anyone? Why doesn't my mom love me? Why doesn't anyone love me? Will anyone ever love me?"

I do know one thing. We're going to do everything humanly possible to help her, and try to rebuild her life (and as we're doing all we humanly can, I'm going to be praying extra hard to God for His help too).

I mean, with all the awful, tough, gut-wrenching questions Dana has facing her tonight, the one question she will never have to ask is — "Can I find hope here?"

I do not consider myself to be a follower,
just a lonely deserted soul in a barbaric city,
who walks his own treacherous path in life.

Written by Brian,
after six months alone
on the street

Chapter 8

"I'm sure you can tell
I'm pretty sick," he said.

"Excuse me, ma'am ... I mean Sister," the ghostly figure said.

"I was wondering if maybe you could tell me how to get to the Statue of Liberty," he said.

"I've hitched all the way from Texas to see it," he said. "And I'd like to see her before I die."

I looked into Fred's hollow, but still stubbornly-alive eyes, and swallowed hard. Standing there, staring into his innocent face, I felt I could almost hear a clock ticking inside Fred's body, painstakingly and inexorably counting down how many final weeks, days and hours he had left to live.

He wasn't dead yet, but Fred knew it was coming, and I knew it and God knew it too. The constant drumbeat of tick, tick, tick seemed to grow louder inside my head.

"I'd love to take you there myself later this week," I said. "It's every bit as beautiful as you've imagined," I said.

I wanted to just take him by the hand and lead him there myself, but I had made a million commitments to a ton of other kids, and I was hoping and praying he'd understand. (I'm almost in awe of how many kids we've been seeing this Lenten season. I think God has been working extra overtime sending kids our way!)

"Oh, that's all right," he said. "I appreciate that. But I think I'll go today.

"I promised my girlfriend back in Texas that I'd send her a photo," he said. "I'd like to make sure I get it to her right away. I don't want to disappoint her," he said.

"It sounds like she means a lot to you," I said, smiling.

He started to speak and then paused. It was like he wanted to tell me yes, but that didn't seem quite enough.

"I really love her, Sister," he said, a couple of tears forming in his eyes. "She's all I got left.

"Except you and this place," he added quickly, in his ever-polite way.

As I looked at him I could almost feel a dagger ripping through my heart. Because I knew he was right....

Fred had come to us just a week ago, a hungry and scared and all-alone 16-year-old "old man" who was so exhausted and tired he could barely lift his legs enough to walk.

For the first few days here he didn't have a whole lot to say. He was too spent to say much. What little he did say came out in dribs and drabs. And it broke our hearts.

"I'm a runaway from Texas," he told us first.

"I don't have any family," he said. "I never knew

my dad, and my mom disappeared two years ago when I was 14," he said.

"I've been living on the street since then," he said.

"I'm sure you can tell I'm pretty sick," he said, almost apologizing for his skinny frame and hollow eyes.

"I have AIDS," he said. "I think I got it from my girlfriend," he said. "I ... I guess ... I guess I had sex too early," he said, almost apologetically. (It's always a little strange and unsettling and yet comforting to hear these words from a kid like Fred. "I wish, I wish, I wish I had known better," his eyes were telling me. I wish every kid could know that truth....)

"But it's not her fault ... she's a nice girl," he said.

"That's why I came to New York," he said. "It's always been my dream to see the Statue of Liberty. I was told ... I was told you would let me stay here for a while," he said.

His words were always spoken quietly and politely, without fanfare or emotion. He told us he was dying the way a kid might tell you, "I'm going outside for awhile," or, "I think I'll check what's on TV tonight."

It wasn't until he said, "I was told you would let me stay here for awhile," that his voice cracked. He said it with real fear, as if he was scared we wouldn't let him stay.

"Of course you're welcome here," I told him when he had asked. "You're welcome to stay with us for-ever," I said, not knowing exactly how long forever might be.

From the second I told Fred he was welcome here — from the second he learned we cared about him, and treasured him and wanted him with us — a transformation took place inside him.

It wasn't as if he was miraculously cured of his disease. We know that will never happen. We took Fred to a doctor, who confirmed that Fred indeed was in the final stages of AIDS and his prognosis was not good. But while we don't know how much time Fred has left on this earth, we do know that as long as he is with us he will feel the love and hope every kid needs. The fact he is dying will never change that.

But inside Fred's heart and soul ... inside I can literally see a transformation reflected in his eyes.

Inside Fred ... something truly miraculous has happened.

The soul that has carried such pain and scars — scars that were formed by rejection, by being abandoned, by feeling unloved and unworthy — has now heard a different message.

By simply letting Fred know that we are here for him, that we care, that we believe he is good and worthy of our love ...

... by giving Fred these simple gifts, we have rekindled a hope that had long ago died in his heart.

I can't overstate how much these words — these words made possible by our love and your support — have meant to Fred.

Quite simply, you have helped give Fred a reason to live.

You have given him a reason to dream.

"I hope you enjoy your visit to the Statue," I said to him before he left. "I know you'll love it," I said, still in awe that this dying boy had just dragged his body 1,500 miles to see our nation's symbol of hope and liberty.

"It's something I've always dreamed of seeing," he said. "I'm glad I made it. I can't wait to tell you about it. Talk to you later," he said.

"And thanks, Sister," he said.

"I really mean it," he said.

With that, he turned around and left. For the first time, I could see a smile on his face. I think I could hear God cheering as well.

I think I know why Fred came to us this past week. I think he was God's Easter present to you and me.

I mean, I think kids like Fred understand Easter — the pain and betrayal of Good Friday, the joy and resurrection of Easter Sunday — better than you or I ever could.

Kids like Fred know more than you or I ever could what it's like to feel totally forsaken, to feel abandoned, to feel betrayed and lost and alone. And to die inside. To them, their entire lifetime has been an endless stream of Good Fridays.

And when their personal resurrection comes? There is absolutely nothing more beautiful in this world, than to be there to see a child like Fred be literally reborn before your eyes.

Sometimes, the resurrection we see is total and

absolute.

A kid who was alone and lost on the street will come to us, and we'll be able to slowly piece his or her life back together. We'll find that kid a new home. We'll find that kid a job. We'll slowly help rebuild every part of a kid's life.

In Fred's case? With Fred, the resurrection has been one inside his heart and his soul. Whether his body lives, and how long it lives, is something I can't answer. But we do know that something deep inside — that need to be loved, that need to feel loved, that absolute need all children have to feel good and worthy and respected and cared about — that something has been reborn inside Fred.

And it's all thanks to you.

I mean, I hope you realize that Fred is God's Easter present to you, too. Kids like Fred simply don't rise out of the quicksand of the street alone. They absolutely need someone to pull them out. Those are your hands that saved Fred this week.

Our Love

Sometimes I wonder how people
    judge our love,
They never seem to notice that it
    comes from Heaven above,
But if our love is strong and true
    and solid to the soul,
Then listening to them is not
    what we'll do.
Our love will be bold.
The love we have will shine
    through storms,
No matter how rough the times.
Forever and ever, we'll be
    together like the sun.
Yes, it will shine.

Written by a
Covenant House kid

Chapter 9

"He used to have this belt he used after he was done drinking at night," he said.

"Hey, Sister," he said. "I've got a few minutes before I have to leave for my job interview. Can I give you a hand?

"There must be something I can do for you to help," he said. "Things are so busy around me.

"Just let me know if there's anything, OK?" he said. "I'll do whatever you want me to do."

He looked up at me, all eager eyes and ears, rocking back and forth on the balls of his feet, as if he were waiting for the beginning of a road race.

In all my years at Covenant House, of all the kids I've met (and I've met a lot of them ... we've seen more than 500,000 the last 26 years!), I've never seen a kid more eager than Jerry. I've never seen a kid more anxious to help. To work. To do. To be happy.

If you had been where Jerry had been, you'd probably understand why....

"I wonder if I could stay here," Jerry had told me a month ago, when he first came to Covenant House.

"I've got nowhere else to go," he said.

"I don't have a father," he told me that first day. "I used to, but he left. But that's OK," he said.

"Because all he did was beat me anyway," he said.

He looked at me, and I could see the muscles begin to pop inside his chin. Some kids, being kids, can exaggerate when they tell me about the lives they've left behind. But the look on Jerry's face told me all I needed to know about his past. I was staring at a kid living a nightmare.

"I'm so sorry, Jerry," I said. "It must have been awful for you."

"It was," he said. "He used to have this belt he used after he was done drinking at night," he said, his eyes beginning to mist. "I hated that belt," he whispered so softly I could barely hear him.

"I was so glad when he ran away that day."

"What about your mother?" I asked.

"I don't have a mother," he said. "I mean, I did, but then she didn't want to be my mother anymore. After my father left, she kind of went off the deep end," he said.

"All she did was sit around the house doing drugs all the time," he said.

"I couldn't take it anymore...

"I couldn't wait to get out," he said.

"Where did you go to?" I asked. "It must have been pretty scary going out on your own," I said.

"I really didn't go anywhere," he said. "I ran out onto the street and walked around for a few days," he said.

"I didn't really know what to do. I ... I begged for food a lot," he said. "I slept outside. I ... I did what I had to do, you know?" he said.

"Then I just decided I needed to do something with my life," he said. "I figured ... I thought if I was going to waste my life I might as well go to someplace like New York," he said. "So I hitchhiked here," he said.

"It hasn't been easy," he said.

From the second Jerry arrived here, he has been like a kid on a mission.

If there's a special workshop on finding a job, he's the first one there at his desk. Right in the front row. Asking questions. Seeking advice. Looking for help — absolutely any help he can find — to make something of his life.

And his energy — the uninhibited, ready-to-burst, wall-to-wall energy of a kid discovering life — is nonstop.

"Can I help you clear the table?" I often hear his voice saying in the cafeteria ... "Is there a new kid you want me to talk to today?" ... "When do you think I can go to my next class?...."

In a world where things come too easily and too early for too many kids, Jerry is working extra hard at succeeding the hard way. He may have been late in discovering the opportunities life has to offer, but he's not going to let that stop him from racing ahead.

He is 17, and he is a kid who has seen the underside of life and desperately wants what else is out there. Like so many of our kids, he is armed with little more than hope and a dream and a burning desire to "be somebody" ... "do something"... "make a life of my own."

And today, just 30 days after he escaped from a "home" life that promised nothing but pain and dead-ends, he is going for his first job interview.

I gave him an extra long hug as he left to chase his dream today. I know Jerry was really happy that you were there with him as he walked out the door this morning.

I mean, everything about Jerry today — from the new clothes he wore to the new hope he carries inside — was there because of you.

You're the one who helped to give him the hope every kid deserves. You're the one who helped take his hand and lead him away from his lonely dead-end street.

Thank you for being there for him and with him.

Thank you for understanding him and caring about him as you do.

I am so very, very proud of him. And so very, very thankful for you.

I truly thank God every day that you found us.

Dear Lord,
Thank you for taking care of me. I never had no
one to care about me. Oh and I'm sorry for what
happened yesterday. Lord, You know why I want
to stay here, because I don't trust anybody on the
streets right now. Danger is always going on. I
wish I could get adopted by a nice person. I've
never been treated nice or like a daughter. Lord
I send wishes for my family and friends.

A prayer written
by a kid in our
Covenant House chapel

Chapter 10

"Thanks," was all she could say.
And that said it all.

It happened again just yesterday.

A young girl knocked on our door at twilight. She had been on the street for six months. She had been abandoned by her father, abused by her stepfather and kicked out of the house by her mother. (An all-too-typical story for our kids.)

She showed up at our door filthy, cold and hungry.

Her eyes held that shell-shocked, terrified look that said, "I know I'm about to be rejected and hurt again." I see that look all too often in kids like her. It was as if the hope part of her heart was dead.

When I said, "Welcome, Cindy. I'm so glad you're here," she stared at me, searching my eyes for the catch.

And then she began to cry. Not the wailing cry of a kid expressing pain. Hers were the other kind of tears.

Her eyes grew soft and then a bit shiny. I could see wetness on her bottom lids and in the corners of her eyes.

Then the drops became rivers as her heart let her trust that I really did care about her and that she was finally safe.

She managed a timid smile as tears ran down her cheeks.

"Thanks," was all she could say. And that said it all.

Have you ever cried those kind of tears? The tears that come from relief? The tears that come from knowing that there is hope again when it all seemed hopeless?

That's what inevitably happens when a kid finally feels he or she has found a chance ... a real chance at life.

Of all the things we do for these kids, letting them know that someone cares about them seems to make the most difference. I think that's what our Covenant with them really is.

Of course, we give our kids all the tangible things they need. We feed them. We put clothes on their backs. We help them find homes and schools and jobs. And on and on and on....

But most of all, most desperately of all, we give them the certain knowledge that they are good and worthwhile and worthy of our love. And that many of us — you, me and God — care.

And when they hear and see and feel that love? It makes many of our kids cry.

It's hard to believe, but so many of our kids have never known that feeling. They've been kicked out, and sometimes just kicked. They've been beaten on and beaten down. They've been sexually abused. They've been emotionally abused.

And when they finally feel safe ... when they finally believe, really believe, that the world might hold some love for them ... their relief is just overwhelming.

I can't tell you how satisfying it is to see ... I can't imagine a more priceless gift to a kid in need.

I can't imagine a better way to turn that first kind of tears we usually see at our doorstep — the tears of pain — into the second kind of tears — the glorious tears of relief and hope.

Thank you for keeping us in your prayers. I never, ever stop thanking God you found us.

Dear Lord,
I believe in You but I am so confused about where
I'm going — all I know is where I've been. I am
so scared and I have no one to talk to but myself
and I hide my feelings in my music.

A prayer written
by a kid in our
Covenant House chapel

Chapter 11

"He said I was not welcome in his house anymore."

"He made me sleep outside in the car every night," he said.

"No matter how cold it was, or how bad it got outside, he said I *had* to sleep in the car," he said.

"He said I wasn't good enough to be in his house."

The young boy looked up at me for a second to let his words sink in and then closed his eyes and shook his head. For the next minute he stood there in front of me like that, periodically opening his mouth to say something, but then sighing and shaking his head a little harder. He was a kid literally having trouble believing the words he was saying....

"I don't understand," I said. "*Who* made you sleep outside every night?"

"It was my stepfather," he said. "He said there was only enough room in the house for two kids ... *his* two kids. He said I was not welcome in his house anymore. He said I was scum."

"Why is he so angry at you?" I asked.

Mitchell opened his eyes slowly for a second and then shut them quickly. His mood, his face, his posture changed instantly before me — a kid transformed from someone who was hurt and angry into someone who was suddenly very insecure and weak and shy.

He bit his lip a half dozen times before he finally looked away and began to speak. The words were so soft, I had to strain to hear them.

"You see, I told my mom one night that I thought there was something wrong with me," he said.

"I told her I thought I was gay.

"As soon as my stepfather heard that, he said I could never sleep inside his house again."

At that, Mitchell opened his eyes for a second to see my reaction and then shut them. A quiet tear began to stream down his cheek.

"What about your mother?" I asked. "Did she try to make your stepfather change his mind?"

"Yeah," he said, softly. "She wanted to stand up for me, but every time she tried my stepfather would beat her. It was really bad, Sister. Really, really bad," he said, his voice barely a whisper.

"I'm very sorry that he acted that way," I said.

"It must have really hurt to be treated like that.

"You're a great kid, Mitchell," I said. "You don't deserve being treated like that," I said.

Mitchell just kept his eyes closed as another tear streamed down his face. He was too choked up at that moment to say anything.

"I wish you were right," his softly shaking head seemed to say.

Some kids close their eyes because they literally want to leave you behind, to go someplace that's their very own. Others close their eyes because they're so unsure and so convinced of their worthlessness that they're afraid to look you in the eye ... even though they desperately need a friend to talk to.

That second look is one I see all the time from kids like Mitchell — kids who are told they are innately bad and unworthy and unloved because they are gay. Ironically, it's these kids that need someone to look in their eyes and talk to them most of all....

"We're really glad you found us, Mitchell," I said.

"How did you end up here?" I asked.

The answer came, as I expected, almost instantly. Mitchell was dying for someone to listen.

"I finally couldn't take it anymore," he said. "So I decided to run away. I walked to the highway, and stuck my thumb out," he said. "I didn't have any idea where I was going. I just knew I had to go somewhere else," he said.

"It was either that, or kill myself," he said.

I knew from Mitchell's eyes that he wasn't exaggerating. The suicide rate for gay kids is much, much higher than for the general population. Imagine how it must be for these kids? To be told, by how they are treated and mistreated, that they are no good and not lovable. If you were told that often enough, especially by the parents you thought loved you, what would you do? How would you survive? Where would you go?

Too often, these kids do the unthinkable.

It's a tragedy that absolutely breaks my heart....

"I'm so glad you didn't hurt yourself," I said.

"You've got so much to offer this world," I said.

"Thanks," his closed eyes said. "I needed to hear that," they said. I think he was too choked up again to get any words out of his mouth.

"What happened next?" I asked.

"I ended up hitchhiking," he said. "I traveled more than a thousand miles 'til I got here. It was pretty awful," he said, trying to smile, but not able to pull it off. "I didn't have any money, I didn't know anybody, I didn't know what to do or where to go ... so I just walked the streets for a week, sleeping in alleys and eating anything I could find.

"Then someone told me about you," he said, actually opening his eyes to look at me.

The look in his eyes was so innocent and beautiful they almost froze me. They literally screamed out in desperation ... "Please help me, I'm a good kid, I don't want to hurt anyone, I just want a chance, I think I deserve one, is there anyone here who will listen to me...."

I put my hand on his shoulder and then reached out and gave him a hug. The sob I heard over my shoulder was one of the saddest I've ever heard. He was one of the most lost kids I've ever met.

"Thanks for listening," he said, looking at me (he finally felt comfortable enough to do that). "I'd like to stay here for a while, if that's all right," he said.

"I'd like that," I said. "You can stay as long as you'd like," I said.

Denise, one of our greatest and most experienced

counselors, took him by the hand and led him to the front desk. I could tell he was going to need help for a long, long time.

"Thanks for helping him find us, God," I whispered. "Thank you."

P.S. I know that some people might feel uncomfortable about the subject of my newsletter this month. But I know that you'd really love Mitchell if you met him. I mean, I see in Mitchell everything I see in all our kids. I don't see a kid who's tall or short, or overweight or thin, or black or white, or boy or girl, or gay or straight. I see a beautiful creation of God, someone who has come to us because he has been denied the basic things every child deserves; the knowledge that he is worthy and good and priceless and loved.

We have 1,400 Covenant House kids under the roofs of all our shelters tonight — in all shapes and sizes, some as young as 10, desperately and urgently needing someone like you to care and guide them.

I'm praying that you might be able to help again now. Please? The need this month is extra urgent!

Thank you and God bless you!

My precious Jesus,
I am hurting. To write everything would fill this
book. You know my troubles, You know my ques-
tions and You know my answers. Please help me.
Give me strength and please give me what I need
to be happy. Please love and take care of my cats
and all the hungry people and creatures of the
world.

> *A prayer written*
> *by a kid in our*
> *Covenant House chapel*

Chapter 12

"He just tried to kill me about two hours ago," she whispered.

"He's trying to kill me," the little girl whispered, barely able to choke the words out.

Long pause.

"He says I belong to him and no one else," she said.

Longer pause.

"I can't believe my father is doing this to me ... it's really bad ... he's ... he's forcing me to have sex with him.

"I can't believe this is really happening."

She looked over to the door, then through the window, then back to the door again. I couldn't catch hold of her eyes — she wouldn't let me. At first I thought that she was simply too ashamed, too racked with guilt and too overcome with self-loathing to look at me. (This devastating self-hatred is common with sexually abused girls — as if what they are doing is *their* fault.)

But when I got up from my chair and she jumped up and started trembling, I knew something else was making Allie's eyes jump across the room — she was absolutely petrified that her father was going to find her.

I quietly sat in the chair next to her and reached out to put my hand on her shoulder. The volunteers who had welcomed her inside our shelter this morning said that she was 15, but I could've sworn she was only about 12. She looked that small and alone. That timid and fragile.

"I'm so sorry about what has happened," I said, trying to talk as softly as I could and still be heard.

"I want you to know you're safe here," I said. "You don't have to be scared any more. We'll protect you."

As I was speaking these last words, the phone rang down the hallway prompting Allie to jerk up and tremble some more. It was like talking to a kid while she was asleep and tossing and turning through a nightmare. Sweat was beginning to bead on her forehead. A snowdrift of shredded tissues, which Allie had twisted and torn apart, rested underneath her chair.

"How do you know?" she finally said while staring at the door. "I mean, he'll do anything to get me. I mean, you have no idea what he'll do," she said, beginning to cry a little harder.

"What do you mean?" I asked the two eyes looking over at the door. "Did something happen today?" I asked. I was almost afraid to hear her answer.

Allie stared at the door for what seemed like an eternity, then slowly shifted her eyes over to me. She had one of those unmistakable "I'm-sure-you're-never-going-to-believe-what-I'm-about-to-tell-you-but-please-I'm-hoping-you-will" looks we receive from the most scared and lost and scarred kids. I reached over and held her hand, urging her to tell me.

"He just tried to kill me about two hours ago," she

whispered. "I ... I came home from school and told him I had a boyfriend. That's when he started to choke me and say I belonged to him," she said.

"I ... I kicked him and crawled through the window and down a fire escape. I heard him jump up and start chasing me. I ... I tried not to look back, but I could hear his feet ... I could hear him yelling after me to come back.

"He said I would never, ever get away."

"I'm afraid he's right," Allie said, weeping softly into her hands. "He's right, isn't he?"

I took a deep breath and squeezed her hand. She's 15 years old and she has been molested and abused by the one person she should be able to trust most in the world (her mother died when she was a baby), and she feels that there is not one single place where she will ever, ever find happiness or peace.

It's the worst kind of pain and rejection we see here at Covenant House. I mean, it's devastating enough when a kid has been abandoned or sent off by a parent who has neither the time nor interest nor desire to love them (and we see thousands and thousands of these kids every year). This kind of betrayal of parental responsibility is heartbreaking enough.

But when a child is violated and then pursued by a parent who wants to hurt her ... when a kid is abused and terrified to the point where she is so traumatized and hyper-vigilant she can't even feel safe at a place like Covenant House ... this is the greatest tragedy of all.

The trauma gripping these kids is so palpable it can

literally leave a bitter taste in my mouth. And please forgive me, God, but I cannot feel love for the parents who do this to their children. I'm sorry, God, but I can't.

"I want you to listen to me," I said to Allie. "I want you to know some things because a great kid like you deserves to know these things," I said. Even though her face was still in her hands, I could tell she was desperately anxious to hear what I had to say.

"First, I want you to know we're very glad you found us and we'll do everything we can to help you. We all care very much about you and want you to feel safe here.

"Second, I want you to know that you are safe here. I promise. I will see to that myself, even if I have to stand guard outside your room 24 hours a day."

Her lips curled a half smile at the thought of me vigilantly blocking the entrance to her room. It was only a hint of a smile, but it was beautiful to see.

"Thanks," she said, twisting another tissue.

"It really means a lot to me ..." she said, beginning to weep all over again.

We sat together quietly for a long time without many words being spoken. She really didn't feel like talking much more (she had cried so much she was just worn out), but she wanted me to stay. And I wanted to stay. I wanted to assure her that she could feel comfortable here and safe here and believe in something or someone here. I think it meant a lot to her.

I don't know what's going to happen next. I do

know that we will never, ever let Allie's father get his hands on her again. Ever! I also know that we will shower Allie with love and do all we can, day by day, bit by bit, to help her begin to understand that she is as precious and worthwhile and worthy of love as any kid in the world. It's going to be a long haul, but thanks to people like you, Allie will feel that sense of joy and self-love someday. I just know it!

Thank you as always for that gift you provide so quietly and faithfully to our kids. I know God smiles more than just a half smile whenever He thinks about what you do for our kids. I know I do, too.

I hope things are well with you and all those you love, particularly those kids in your life who aren't Covenant House kids. While you say a prayer for ours tonight, we will all be praying for yours as well....

Run Away

Scared and cold,
first night on the streets

Your body hurts
from your head to your feet

You miss school,
not the work — it's the friends

Thinking what you'll say
when they ask
where you've been

Gotta dollar-fifty,
every penny gotta spend

Make a wrong move ... Boom —
your life comes to an end.

> *Daniel, 16*
> *a kid on the street*

Chapter 13

"My parents died when I was in the first grade," he told me.

If those singing angels came to Covenant House this Christmas, I think they'd feel right at home.

You remember the singing angels, don't you? They sang to the shepherds in the fields, "Do not be afraid; for behold, I proclaim to you good news of great joy!"

The "Do not be afraid" part is something every homeless kid yearns to hear from us. Indeed, it's the first message that we give to our kids on Christmas Eve — and the first part of the miracle that transforms our kids at Christmas.

You see, the kids who live on the street and come to Covenant House at Christmas — and we'll see 1,400 of them in all — know more about fear than maybe any other kids on earth.

It's not so much the fear of physical punishment. As painful as it might be to hear (and as awful as it feels to say), beatings and suffering are a constant presence in a homeless kid's life.

What our kids really fear at Christmas — a fear that is so searing you can see it literally screaming from their eyes — is the fear that they will be alone during the Christmas season. That they will be without someone to talk to. Someone to love them. Again.

So, when we see our kids on Christmas Eve, we tell them not to be afraid.

"It's OK. You're safe now," I tell them.

They really need to hear that.

Of course, simply letting our kids know they needn't be afraid is only half of the healing miracle that takes place at Christmas.

It's that special and wonderful moment when our kids actually feel the joy that makes Covenant House so very special at Christmas.

On Christmas Eve, I'll again stand at the door and see some of the same kinds of kids — hurting, alone, infinitely beautiful — I see every Christmas Eve. I'll see a disheveled and desperate boy, like the one I met last year.

"I just got off the bus," he told me last Christmas Eve. "My parents beat me. I had to get away," he said. "I ... I'm alone ... I'm cold ... can I, could you let me stay with you?" he asked.

"Of course," I said. "Please come in. I'm glad you found us," I said (even though it hurt to say that because all the time I was wishing he was home, spending time with a family that loved him and wanted him).

At that moment, I saw something else in his eyes besides pain. "Maybe ... just maybe someone cares," his eyes said. "Maybe she means it," they said.

The pure joy wasn't there in his heart just yet, but the seeds of that joy were planted. The angels saw to that....

Then a young girl, pregnant, will come to the door this year, just like the one who came last Christmas Eve.

"I made a mistake and got pregnant," she told me. "My dad got so mad he beat me up and I ran away. I've been on the streets for months and I'm so tired. Please, please can I stay here tonight?" she asked.

"Please, come in," I said, as I hugged her. "You're welcome here." And as I led her inside, she wiped away her tears and whispered a "thank you," too tired and too ashamed to even look me in the eyes. At that moment, I felt I could actually see the Christmas miracle begin to grow in her heart, too....

And I'm sure that once again, long after dinnertime and well into the night, I'll see another scared and aimless boy, like the 16-year-old kid who knocked on our door last Christmas Eve.

"My parents died when I was in the first grade," he told me. "I lived with an alcoholic aunt who beat me and threw me out when I was 12," he said. The boy would have stared at me in bewilderment if I told him about joy that night, but the angels made sure <u>he</u> felt the miracle, too.

If there is any proof needed that God cares about these kids, it's that by Christmas Eve dinnertime, kids will be here in droves.

And thanks to you, we'll all be here waiting. Ready to give them a Christmas they've never known, but desperately need to feel.

This Christmas Eve, we'll shower these kids with good food and clean clothes, and smother them with love (knowing all the while we can never, ever be as good as the real thing). We'll stand hand in hand with them and we'll sing carols together. We'll hug each other a hundred times, and tell stories to each other, and share that magical Christmas Eve love with each other.

Each kid at Covenant House will open their gifts and go to sleep feeling — truly feeling down deep in their souls — a tranquility they may have never felt before on Christmas Eve.

In the dark and stillness, the miracle will happen — a Christmas miracle.

And in the morning the Christ Child will be born again ... in the faces of our kids.

Their problems won't have disappeared. The miracle of Christmas doesn't work like that. But there will be something different, even if only for one day....

The boy who felt no one cared about him last year? He woke up Christmas morning with a new light in his eyes. The young girl who came to us in tears, was crying again last Christmas morning. But this time, she was crying quiet tears of joy.

This year, once again, every kid without a home will stand near our Christmas tree and be surrounded by a truly loving family. And somehow, the Christmas carols will sound like hymns of joy such as you've never heard before.

I wish you could be here then ... to see the miracle. To see God in each of their faces.

You would truly see the real spirit of Christmas then. Not a "Ho, Ho, Ho," kind of spirit, but the real unbridled joy of a cold, dark world being lit by the Star of Bethlehem.

Christmas is not easy here. <u>Yet, Christmas here is the best way I have actually experienced God's gift to the world</u>.

<u>Of course, all of it is possible because of you</u>. The Christmas miracle of Covenant House simply wouldn't happen without you. That's why my first prayer on Christmas morning is always one of thanks that you found us. Always....

Maybe you could do me a favor this Christmas. Whenever you hear someone say, "I wish Christmas would last all year," think of my kids and say a prayer for them.

Pray that God gives them the peace and joy and acceptance they find around the tree on Christmas morning at Covenant House.

Pray that Christmas morning will be the start for them of something that can last all through the year. That they will realize in their hearts — even if they can't understand it yet in their heads — that the Christ Child came to earth for them.

That will be my Christmas prayer this year. The rest of the year I'll continue to thank God that you found us.

*"The running never stops. You run from
the drugs; you run from the pimps; you
run from the police; you run from every-
body, and you just keep running. Well,
I'm tired of running."*

> Allison, 16, now safely in
> a Covenant House shelter

Chapter 14

*"Daddy, I kept
dreaming you'd come
and save me," she said.*

"Sister, I can't do this. Please. I'm just too scared."

Beth thrust the phone towards me and turned away.

"Beth, it's all right," I said, "You don't have to call right now. We can do this later."

Beth's head swung back around and her eyes opened wide. She pulled the phone back to her and clutched it to her chest.

"You don't understand. If I call him ... you know ... I mean, if I call him...."

"What? Beth. What will happen?"

She looked at me and her eyes softened. She hugged the phone even closer, and I heard it switch from a dial tone to that recording that says, "We're sorry, your call did not go through."

Beth didn't seem to notice.

"It's just that for the last three weeks, the only thing that kept me from killing myself after Mark beat me or raped me was thinking that my daddy would save me."

A tear formed in the corner of her eye, but she didn't cry.

"I kept thinking how wrong I had been. I thought

my father was the enemy. I really did. And I thought Mark was my friend.

"Sister, how could I have been so wrong?"

I wanted to stop her then. I wanted to tell her not to be so hard on herself. That she was far from the first kid who made that mistake. Far from the first girl who was convinced to run away from her home.

Mark was in his 20s. Beth was 14. She ran away from home a month ago and came to the city to be with Mark. A week after they arrived he began beating her and telling her she was trash. And he began raping her.

Was Beth naive? Was she stupid?

You could probably say "yes" to both those questions. But I will tell you that she is not alone. Our streets are full of kids who run away from home — something that will happen a million times this year! — and then become trapped by predators like Mark.

I'm just glad she finally managed to call 911. The police brought her here this morning. I hope they find Mark.

She might have been dead in another week. Or tomorrow.

"How could I have been so wrong?" Beth repeated.

Then she held the phone out in front of her and stared at it. "Sister, what if I call him and he won't talk to me? What if he says, 'NO. You can't come home!' What if he hates me now?"

I wanted to tell Beth that none of those things would happen. Unfortunately, I wasn't sure. Sometimes parents do react that way when a child runs away and then wants to come home again. It's one of the saddest things I've ever seen.

"I don't know, Beth," I said. "I hope it's okay. Maybe it will take a little time. Sometimes it takes a little time. In any case, you're welcome here. You know that."

Beth looked at me and the tears welled up again.

"I know that, Sister. Thank you."

She put the phone to her ear, heard the recording and reset it. Then she dialed. It seemed like forever before she said, "Daddy? Daddy? It's me Bethie! Daddy, I'm so sorry."

I don't know exactly what Beth's father said. All I could hear was Beth's end. For 10 minutes, she went on with variations of "No, it's all MY fault." "I'm so sorry, Daddy." "I miss you, too." "I know. I was scared, too." "Daddy, I kept dreaming you'd come and save me." "I know. I know you love me."

It was a two-tissue-box phone call.

I want to thank you for that two-tissue-box phone call. I want to thank you on behalf of Beth and her father. I said a special prayer for you after that phone call.

Beth's father is on his way to the airport already. He'll be here in a couple of hours to take his daughter home. Beth's mother died when she was young and she and her father have had a rocky time in the last few years. But that phone call convinced me that they love and need each other. I'm sure they're going to be OK. Thanks again for helping us to be here for her.

Epilogue

I started this book by saying that it was a good thing that God has good ears. Now I want to add that it's a good thing so many kind and generous people have good ears as well.

It never ceases to amaze me how people respond when I tell them about our kids. I mean, let's face it, though I swear that my kids are beautiful inside, it's sometimes hard to see it on the outside.

These are street kids. They are often dirty. They are often tough. They have built up a protective shell so thick that some people just can't face them.

But I thank God every single day that some people can get by all that gritty street kid stuff and listen to the children underneath.

I thank God every day that some people have the ability to hear the pleas of these kids and respond, not just with, "Oh, that's really awful," but with action and true concern.

I thank God every day that when I keep asking and asking for help, so many people respond. Nothing amazes me more.

So I hope you are one of those people. I hope you have listened to my kids and that you like them. They are so likable underneath it all.

I hope you will want to help because I really do need it. It is a monumental task to find the money to support so many crisis centers. And the job we do is one that no one else seems to want.

I honestly believe that God chose Covenant House to answer the prayers of His kids. He put us here and He keeps the doors open so that when it's dark and quiet and another precious child is crying, "God, please save me," God has a place to send them.

I once thought I'd have this problem licked by now — after all, I'm 70 and I've been at this for over 50 years. But I have found that being here ... being the one to whom God sends those children that He hears in the night ... is more exciting, more satisfying, more right than anything else I have ever done in my life.

Please join me. You'll never regret it!

Sister Mary Rose

"I bound myself by oath,
I made a covenant with you ...
and you became mine."

Ezekiel 16:8

(Our oath, the first thing kids see
when they walk into our shelter.)

Faith Into Action

Your invitation to join the
Covenant House Faith Community

By now you know that Covenant House is more than a shelter for kids — it's a mission inspired by, led by and dedicated to God. For some very special people, just reading about our kids is not enough. They want to be part of this work, to see and feel first hand what our kids go through.

It's for these people that the Covenant House Faith Community was created.

Our Faith Community is a group of full-time volunteers who put their faith into action by dedicating 13 months of their lives to the mission of Covenant House. These extraordinary people come from all walks of life, from every corner of the country. They are as young as 21 and as old as their mid-70s. But as different as they are, they all share a common purpose — to make our kids' world, and all our worlds, a better place than they found it. Community members live together in prayer and service to God and to the kids of Covenant House. Faith Community volunteers combine a faith-motivated giving of themselves with a deep commitment to serving Covenant House kids.

This commitment to adolescents and young adults

who are homeless is a true expression of the gospel and an enriching experience for members of the Faith Community. A life combining prayer and community life becomes a support to the service commitment and an opportunity to reflect and grow spiritually and personally. If you are over 21 years old, please consider joining this special group of people.

"Up until last year I was a perfectly normal graduate student, getting my Ph.D. and studying urban poverty ... now I work with girls who were pregnant at 16 and kids my little brother's age who sold and used drugs while my brother was still running a paper route," says Ann, a Faith Community member. *She adds, "I come home so exhausted, I cannot see straight ... it's been the best year of my life."*

Please read on as two more Faith Community volunteers share their stories....

Missy

"I know it sounds corny," says Missy, *"but I believe it was my destiny to come to Covenant House."*

"I first heard about Covenant House when my high school youth group (from Whitehall, PA) came for a tour in my freshman year. The tour of Covenant House gave me the idea of becoming a social worker. As the years went by, I received fund-raising letters from Covenant House and majored in Social Work at Ohio State University. In my senior year, I read about the Faith Community at Covenant House in *Choices* (a booklet about full-time volunteer opportunities). I came for the Orientation — and I knew I had to join.

"I came to New York in September of 1995, to join a community I wasn't even sure I would fit into. My experience started with Formation, an extensive three-week program of workshops and sessions. I was suddenly spending all my time looking at myself. Where was I with my faith? How did I deal with others? How would I handle hostility or rejection from the kids? Was I up to loving and living in a community? How would I live a simple life, chastely, and with little money?

"I was making a commitment to pray daily with people I didn't know. I was making a commitment, I realized later, to love unconditionally. It was overwhelming — the first three weeks of non-stop self-examination. And in the back of my mind was the fear, 'Would I be able to work with the Covenant House kids?'

"When Formation was over, I was ready to get to work. I wanted to work in the Community program, a Covenant House storefront, which brings education and vocation services to the neighborhood. I liked it because such programs, it seemed to me, could keep kids where they lived and prevent them from ever having to go to the crisis center.

"My first job at Covenant House was as a Resident Advisor in the crisis center, working with our young girls. There are about 35–40 young women at any given time. When I interviewed for the position (yes, even though I was a volunteer, I had to interview like

any other staff member would), I was asked the exact
question I had been asking myself during the three
weeks of Formation: 'What makes you think you can
do this kind of work?' 'I don't know,' I said. 'I only
know I want to learn.'

"For the first few weeks I spent most of my time
observing. Gradually, I began to get a case load. I was
assigned as a Counselor to new kids as they came in. It
was difficult at first because I was intimidated by the
rough exterior the kids sometimes have (it's a defense
mechanism by kids who have been hurt so often they
can't trust anyone). What was really hard for me was
to be direct and to put myself in a position where I
might have to say no. I didn't know what would happen if I did. I was afraid.

"Naturally, I am not very assertive. I am a nice
person who wants others to be nice, too. But with the
encouragement of my supervisor, I began to take risks.
I began to get 'in their faces.' To say yes, no. To set
limits and to hold them. At the same time I was growing more confident, I also developed a sense of humor
and an ability to joke around which helped me (and I
think the kids) enormously.

"Working at the crisis center turned out to be a
very good testing ground because of the intensity and
the diversity of the staff and residents. I got stretched
and challenged constantly.

"It was the first Christmas I ever spent away from
my family. I dreaded it. However, it turned out to be
the best Christmas I ever had. We started out with a

prayer service, a wonderful breakfast and then the kids opened presents. For many, it was the first Christmas where they got attention. Many couldn't believe how many gifts they received, and how nice the gifts were. 'This is the best Christmas of my life, and I have never received so many gifts,' they all said. One kid gave all the stuff she had to some other homeless people who gather on 41st St. I was amazed.

"After eight months at the crisis center, I had the opportunity to go to work at the Community Center. At the end of my year, there was an open position and I was hired as a Caseworker. No matter who walks in our doors, we help them, either directly, or with a referral.

"While there were many challenges and growing pains in the work with the kids, I found the Faith Community to be very supportive. I was very fortunate to be able to come to eight other community members and share experiences. Many days I was frustrated and exhausted. Other days I had joys to share, and I could be supportive of others. The work changed me; the Community supported me. I made dear friends. And I fell in love with New York.

"Did I make a difference? Yes. Yes, I believe I did. I started off the year anxious to help, but then I discovered that it wasn't my doing or my helping, but simply my being present. Just being there, that is the doing."

Sally
"I feel something I never felt before."

"I've been in the Covenant House Faith Community for two months. Why didn't I do this 20 years ago? It feels like exactly what I should be doing.

"For 12 years I worked my way up the ladder in the advertising profession. As a Marketing Manager, I found myself pretty much at the top of my specialty and grew bored with it. More money could be made. I could be a Vice President. I could tell more people what to do. But the creative part, the brainstorming, was missing. The higher you go, the less that kind of creativity is part of your job. I had been away from the Church, too. Something was definitely missing in my life.

"I found myself reaffirming my spiritual values, including living the gospel. A Jesuit led me to explore the gospel, which forced me to look at my lifestyle. I could not ignore something that said I needed to look beyond my own door. On a retreat at a monastery, Sister Mary Rose's *Are You Out There, God?* book appealed to me. When I asked about the volunteer program, I told myself I was just curious. Then I found myself coming to New York for an orientation. The Director of the Faith Community was very supportive. It seemed that slowly but deliberately, I was being led to a major change.

"I struggled for a year with my own unwillingness to volunteer. It meant going into a totally new situation, leaving the comfort of my income, my house, my friends. Working through my own inertia was a long process, but a force had been set in motion that I knew couldn't be denied.

"Now that I'm here, I feel something I never felt before, even at the most exciting moments of working in the advertising world, which is a sense of peace and a sense of integration. I'm in touch with a deeper part of myself. I'm doing what my heart has led me to do, rather than putting it off for later. I have a sense of being a whole person, even though I'm sometimes overwhelmed.

"Recently I spent a day agonizing about this kid Joe who might have to go back to Rikers (a New York City prison) because he was suspended from Covenant House for fighting. I found myself thinking, 'I can't deal with this kid's pain,' but somehow I was dealing with it. How is it that you can be happy, at peace and disturbed at the same time? I don't know. But it all happens together, and it's a different way of living. I think I'm hooked!

"I get more than I give because these kids are incredibly strong — what they've been through is unbelievable and the fact that they're still functioning is remarkable. Joe's mother died in his arms of asthma when he was 12 years old, and he lived on the street since then selling drugs. I'm surprised he didn't go completely out of his mind.

"Joe had a court date last week. I wrote a letter to the court on his behalf, and they agreed to give him another chance. He's staying with his sister during his 30-day suspension from Covenant House and contin-ues to come to classes and workshops here each day.

After a month, he can come back into Covenant House, and we can tell the court that we're doing OK. They were wonderfully cooperative.

"This experience is part of my own healing. When the love comes through, it heals not only who we work with, but it heals me, in ways that I don't need to understand. Today I felt really happy. I didn't have any reason to feel happy. We started singing songs with this one kid on the elevator and just felt this joy. There was no reason for it.

"In the Faith Community, we live a three-part commitment — prayer, whatever our connection to God is, community and service. That's the commitment we make for 13 months. When you know other people who have made that commitment, that knowledge is very supportive. We pray together morning and evening. Wednesday nights we have dinner, a meeting and Mass together. We care about each other. I was concerned that I wouldn't find things in common with much younger people, but that's not been true at all. There's also someone in Community now who's 75 years old.

"I have many good friends back in California, but this is on a new level. I didn't choose any of these people, but I couldn't have made a better choice, which is really kind of strange....

"From the giving you receive."

Where do we go from here?

My newsletters tell an incredible story ... but they only tell part of the story. Wrapped around the letters I wrote to my friends, I've also included words written to me by others — poems and prayers written by our kids, and letters sent to me by donors who were moved by what they see happening in America today.

And almost every word in this book — whether they were penned by me, a runaway kid, a nervous grandmother, or a teenager in school — carries a consistent message: the American family is falling apart. And we must, each of us, do what we can to repair it. Now!

I passionately believe the breakdown of the family unit is the single deepest ethical and moral challenge of our generation. Whether we respond to it will depend on the resolve and willingness of all of us to commit ourselves to the care and protection of family life. The time for repairing endangered families and rescuing their children is not after they have fallen apart!

The question then is ... how? How can each of us make a difference in repairing the American family? And how can we begin to make that difference now?

Because the survival of the family is so very important to our futures, we have prepared a special Family Survival Guide which can be found on the following pages. This Guide features the best things we've learned over the years working with hundreds of thousands of kids, as well as good, time-tested values that we never let ourselves forget. We hope you will share these pages with a parent you know who may need help. Thank you!

Family
Survival
Guide

Reflections on
Raising Kids Today

Values – Teaching Them in Today's World.

Communicating your values has never been more important than it is today. And the good news is, it all begins and ends with you.

When all is said and done, parents have far more influence over instilling values in their kids than any other factor.

Here are some simple, and very important, things we should all remember about values, and passing them along:

- Kids get their sense of what's right and wrong from people they love and respect. No one has more influence over teaching values than you do. Your input can make all the difference!

- When it comes to teaching values ... action *always* speaks louder than words. Kids today have a "show me" mentality. They need to see the values lived out by you. Respect for life, respect for other people, honesty, integrity ... kids get those from watching you. The old saw has never been more true ... children *do* learn what they live!

- Families are still the best vehicle for raising children. A loving, nurturing family unit, of whatever form, creates the kind of environment kids need to learn what's right and wrong ... and how to love themselves too. Values are best inculcated in an environment of love and acceptance.

- Always take time to sit and talk to your kids. Don't be afraid to say what you feel (but don't ever be too closed to listen to what your kids think).

- Always strive to teach your kids to love and respect themselves as children of God. A healthy love and respect for themselves is incredibly important for any kid. It's also the first essential step in helping a kid also learn a love and respect for those around him, and God.

- Nobody has said it better than Jesus. Those three words, "Love Thy Neighbor...." are an important message for every kid!

You've Got a Tough Job.

Most of us were never taught to be parents. So we can't help but disappoint ourselves sometimes. How often have you heard yourself using the very words you hated hearing from your own parents?

And when our kids become teenagers, it gets even harder. They seem to reject everything we've taught them. As far as they're concerned, we know nothing. Our values and beliefs are constantly challenged. Every word we utter is seen as interference. Emotions run high.

But we're more important to our teens than ever. As they try out the values of their peers, who are more influential than ever, we counter the pull of drugs and alcohol. These entangle children every day and can ruin their lives.

The Stakes Are High.

Teenagers who don't get what they need at home look elsewhere. Some run away from home. Many more consider other ways of running from pressure — a once bright and happy son escapes to drugs, a vivacious daughter starts drinking. Think about these facts:

- Each year, one million students drop out of high school or are chronically truant.
- Four out of 10 teenage girls will become pregnant before age 20.
- Although marijuana use has declined in the past years, addiction to cocaine, especially crack, has doubled.
- One in four teens develops a drinking problem during his teen years; about 10,000 will die in alcohol-related accidents this year.
- Each year, 5,000 to 6,000 teens die in suicide-related deaths, and the number is growing, one every 90 minutes. For every death, at least 100 other young people attempt suicide.

The Turbulent Teens.

Teens face many pressures that adults don't take seriously. Their bodies are changing — they have to adjust to the new person they see in the mirror. They feel different. They become interested in sex.

Self-doubt is constant. They feel pressure to conform and fear ridicule if they don't.

These changes can be bewildering, frightening and even depressing.

Teens can have remarkable insights. But they also surprise us with their lack of good judgment.

Your Teen Needs You.

At the time teenagers are crying out to be treated as adults, they also need a nurturing home, a refuge. And though they deny it passionately, they need structure, limits, lots of help sorting out their lives and most important, love.

In the turbulence of growing up, it is important for us parents to remember (even if our teens seem to forget) that we love each other. In the end, that's what makes the whole struggle worthwhile.

How Well Do You Know Your Kids?

You may say, "My teenager wouldn't do that." Most don't. But even if yours wouldn't, think about the following questions:

* Where is your child right now?
* What are your teen's deepest fears?
* Who is your son or daughter's best friend?
* Do your teen's friends feel welcome in your home?

Remember, a strong relationship with your children is the best way for you to guide them, and to prevent them from becoming a sorry statistic.

Getting Along With Your Teen.

Here are some ideas and techniques you can try to improve your relationship with your teen. If they don't work at first, keep trying. They take practice.

1. Make time for your teen. Find an activity you enjoy doing together and pursue it. If your invitations are declined, keep asking.

2. Listen, really listen. Because parents have so much to do and so little time, we often try to listen while cleaning, washing dishes or fixing the car. Put your chores aside so your teen knows you're really paying attention.

3. Take the long view. Don't treat minor mishaps as major catastrophes. Choose the important issues. Don't make your home a battleground.

4. Tolerate differences. View your teenager as an individual distinct from you. This doesn't mean you can't state your opinion if you disagree.

5. Respect your teenager's privacy. If a behavior is worrying you, speak up.

6. Let your teens sort things out themselves. Never say that you know how your teen feels. They believe their feelings (so new and personal) are unique. They'll learn otherwise — without your help. And never imply that their feelings don't matter or will change. Because teens live in the present, it doesn't matter that they'll soon feel differently.

7. Don't judge. State facts instead of opinions when

you praise or criticize. Stating facts like "Your poem made me smile," or "This report card is all Cs and Ds!" leaves it up to your teen to draw the appropriate conclusions. Teens are sensitive about being judged — positively as well as negatively.

8. Be generous with praise. Praise your child's efforts, not just accomplishments. And don't comment on the person. "You're a great artist" is hard to live up to. "I loved that drawing" is a fact and comes from your heart.

9. Set reasonable limits. Teens need them. Your rules should be consistently applied — and rooted in your deepest beliefs and values.

10. Teach your teen to make sensible decisions and choices by encouraging independence and letting your teenager make mistakes. Don't step in unless you have to.

How to Make Anger Work.

All parents get furious at their children. We can't help it. But some parents feel bad about being angry and keep quiet. Though it's easy to say things in anger that you don't mean, anger can also spark talks that will help you and your teen get to know each other better.

Some Guidelines.

• When you get mad, don't blame or accuse. Say how you *feel* — annoyed, irritated, upset, etc. —

and why. Be specific. Talk facts. Blaming only forces a teen to argue his point, arouses tempers, and kills dialogue.

- Think solution, not victory. Don't try to win arguments.
- Stick to the present incident. Fighting old battles will only aggravate a situation.
- Be careful not to attack your teen's person or character. Say, "I'm furious that you didn't clean up after the mess you made" — *not,* "You're a lazy slob!" Your son or daughter may give up trying to improve.
- If the situation is touchy, put your ideas in a letter. You can say exactly what you mean — and your teen will have time to think it over before answering.

Signs That Your Child Needs Outside Help.

- Suicidal talk of any kind. A suicidal teen may also give away valued possessions, make a will, talk about death or dying or say his family would be better off without him.
- Recent changes in sleeping or eating habits, thinking patterns, personality, friendships, study habits, activities. A sudden unexplained end to a long depression often precedes a suicide attempt. Major weight loss can be a sign of bulimia or anorexia — dangerous problems.
- Drug or alcohol use. You might notice: irrational

or irresponsible behavior, lying, secretiveness, severe mood swings, a sudden increase in accidents. A teen with a problem may have dilated pupils or wear sunglasses indoors, or complain about not sleeping or not feeling well. Valuables may disappear. You may find drug paraphernalia or alcohol containers around the house.

- A recent change in friends who you feel may be involved with drugs or alcohol may indicate that your child is involved or be a sign that your child is having other problems.

- Law-breaking behavior, even if the police and courts aren't involved. You might notice new possessions and money not accounted for.

- Poor self-image. Doubts are normal. But persistently low self-esteem is a problem.

- Serious depression. Listlessness, loneliness, withdrawal, difficulty making friends.

- Rebelliousness to the point of total, continual defiance.

- Problems at school, including class-cutting, absenteeism, a sudden drop in grades.

- Fears or anxieties that interfere with everyday activities.

- Problems between family members that aren't solved by listening and discussing. In fact, family changes such as a death, divorce or remarriage are times when teens often need some outside help.

When to Get Help For Yourself.

- Things aren't going well with your family but you can't figure out why.

- You disagree totally with positions your spouse has taken on issues concerning your teen and the two of you can't find a compromise.

- You have trouble holding a job.

- You are abusing drugs or alcohol.

- You get violent with your teenager and can't control yourself.

- Your spouse gets violent with you or your child.

What to Do If Your Teen Runs Away.

Most kids who run away return within 48 hours. Those who stay away can find themselves in many dangerous situations. So do everything you can to bring your child home.

- Keep a notebook recording steps you've taken and dates.

- Check in with: neighbors, relatives, and your teen's friends, teachers, employer or co-workers.

- Contact local hangouts and hospitals.

- Call the police. Have an officer come to your house to take a report and pick up recent photos, dental records and fingerprints if available. Get his name; badge number and phone number; the police report number; and the name of the officer who will follow up.

- Make sure the police lists your teen in the National

Crime Information Center (NCIC) to the state clearinghouse on missing children, if there is one in your state.

- Contact the National Center for Missing and Exploited Children for help with law enforcement officials — 1-800-843-5678.
- Call the Covenant House NINELINE for support and to check for messages. Leave a message. Also check with any local runaway hotlines.
- Contact runaway shelters locally and in nearby states.
- Make posters with photos of your teen, listing: age, height, weight, hair and eye color, complexion, physical characteristics (such as scars, birthmarks, braces or pierced ears), circumstances of disappearance, your phone number and police contacts. Distribute these to truck stops, youth-oriented businesses, hospitals, law-enforcement agencies.
- Be prepared for the first conversation with your teen. Whether in person or by phone, show concern, not anger. Say, "I love you."
- Prepare to quickly begin resolving the problems which caused your child to leave home. When your child returns home, emotions are likely to run high. Someone outside your family can help you all deal with these emotions. You may find that planned time for your teen in a temporary residence or shelter is necessary while you are resolving problems. So get outside help from a trained counselor.

Need expert help or support?

Call our NINELINE counselors at 1-800-999-9999.

We'll put you in touch with people who can help you right in your hometown.

1-800-999-9999

This call is free.

Covenant House
346 West 17th Street
New York, NY 10011-5002

Covenant House Alaska
609 F Street
Anchorage, AK 99501

Covenant House California
Los Angeles:
1325 N. Western Avenue
Hollywood, CA 90027-5611

Oakland:
in formation

Covenant House Florida
Fort Lauderdale:
733 Breakers Avenue
Fort Lauderdale, FL 33304-4196

Orlando:
888 N. Orange Avenue
Orlando, FL 32801

Covenant House Michigan
4151 Seminole Street
Detroit, MI 48214

Covenant House Missouri
in formation

Covenant House New Jersey
Atlantic City:
3529 Pacific Avenue
Atlantic City, NJ 08401

Newark:
14 William Street
Newark, NJ 07102

Covenant House New Orleans
611 North Rampart Street
New Orleans, LA 70112-3540

Covenant House New York
460 West 41st Street
New York, NY 10036

Covenant House Texas
1111 Lovett Boulevard
Houston, TX 77006-3898

Covenant House Washington
3400 Martin Luther King, Jr. Ave., S.E.
Washington, DC 20032

Covenant House Toronto
20 Gerrard Street East
Toronto, Ontario
Canada M5B2P3

Covenant House Vancouver
575 Drake Street
Vancouver, British Columbia
Canada V6B4K8

Covenant House Guatemala
3a Avenida 11–28, 5to piso
Zona 1
Guatemala City, Guatemala

Covenant House Honduras
Apartado 2401
Tegucigalpa, D.C., Honduras

Covenant House Mexico
Paseo de la Reforma 111
Mexico DF 06300, Mexico

Covenant House Nicaragua
Apartado 15
Managua, Nicaragua

Covenant House Donor Assistance Line: 1-800-388-3888
Visit our website at: http://www.CovenantHouse.org

Covenant House is a member of America's Charities, a nonprofit federation that represents a variety of national charities in workplace giving campaigns. To find out if your employer is a part of America's Charities call us at: (800) 458-9505.

Copies of our financial and operating reports have been filed with the state and are available on request. To obtain one, simply write: New York State Department of State, Charities Registration Section, 162 Washington Avenue, Albany, NY 12231 or Covenant House, JAF Box 2973, New York, NY 10116-2973.

West Virginia residents may obtain a summary of the registration and financial documents from the Secretary of State, State Capitol, Charleston, WV 25305. Registration does not imply endorsement.

A copy of the official registration and financial information may be obtained from the Pennsylvania Department of State by calling, toll free, within Pennsylvania, 1-800-732-0999. Registration does not imply endorsement.

Registration and financial documents are available from the Maryland Secretary of State, State House, Annapolis, MD 21401. Registration does not imply endorsement.

For more information or for a copy of our audited financial statement, contact the Executive Director of Covenant House Florida.

or

A copy of the official registration and financial information may be obtained from the Division of Consumer Services by calling 1-800-435-7352 toll-free, within the state. Registration does not imply endorsement, approval or recommendation by the state.

Just a reminder....
Many companies match their employees' charitable donations. Please check with your company or your spouse's company. It could mean extra help for our kids.

Please Help Me, God

Covenant House depends almost entirely on gifts from friends like you to help 48,000 homeless and runaway children every year. We provide food, clothing, shelter, medical attention, educational and vocational training and counseling to kids with no place to go for help. Please help if you can.

YES! I want to help the kids at Covenant House. Here is my gift of: ☐ $10 ☐ $20 ☐ $25 ☐ Other

Name _____

Address _____

City _____ State _____ Zip_____

Please make your check payable to Covenant House.
Your gift is tax deductible.

☐ *Please send me your financial information.*

☐ Please send me _____ copies of *God, Please Save Me*.

Many people like to charge their gift. If you would like to, please fill out the information below:
I prefer to charge my:
☐ American Express   ☐ MasterCard   ☐ Discover   ☐ Visa

Account # _____

Amount _____ Exp. Date _____

Signature_____

Mail to: Covenant House
JAF Box 2973
New York, NY 10116-2973

Or, call 1-800-388-3888 to charge your gift on your
American Express, MasterCard, Discover or Visa.   COUPON